2006 Census Update
to accompany

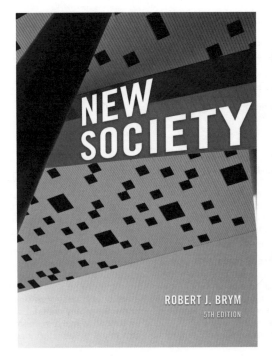

Robert J. Brym
University of Toronto

NELSON EDUCATION

NELSON / EDUCATION

2006 Census Update to accompany
New Society, **Fifth Edition, and**
Sociology: The Points of the Compass

by Robert J. Brym

Associate Vice President, Editorial Director:
Evelyn Veitch

Editor-in-Chief:
Anne Williams

Executive Editor:
Laura Macleod

Senior Marketing Manager:
David Tonen

Developmental Editor:
Sandy Matos

Permissions Coordinator and Photo Researcher:
Melody Tolson

Senior Content Production Manager:
Natalia Denesiuk Harris

Proofreader:
Wendy Yano

Production Coordinator:
Ferial Suleman

Design Director:
Ken Phipps

Managing Designer:
Franca Amore

Interior Design:
Iris Glaser

Compositor:
Zenaida Diores

Printer:
Maracle Press

table of CONTENTS

Data used by permission of Statistics Canada
http://www12.statcan.ca/english/census06/release/index.cfm

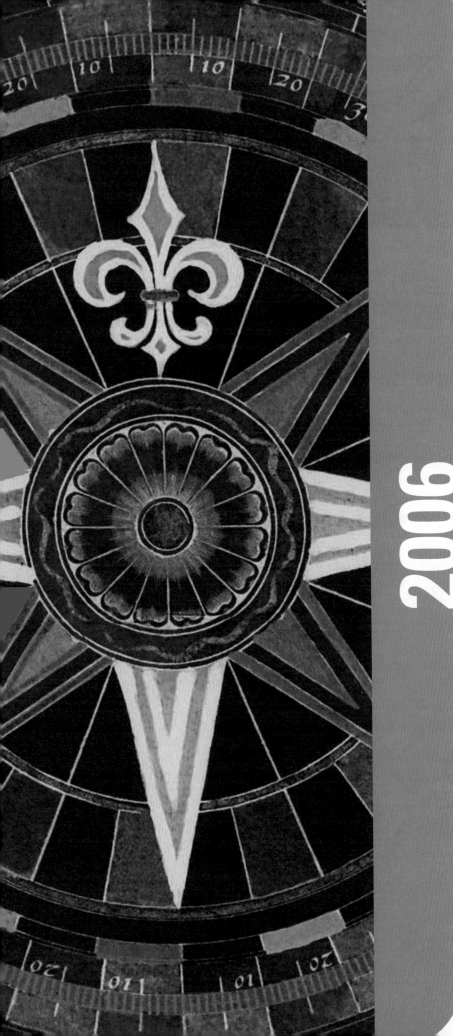

2006 CENSUS UPDATE

Canadian Society and the 2006 Census

Canadian Society and the 2006 Census

Source: Nikolay Okhitin/Shutterstock

The Politics of the Canadian Census

It may seem odd to say so, but the census is one of the most political documents produced by the Canadian government. Often seen as a dry, scientific compilation of numbers of interest mainly to bureaucrats and bean-counters, the census is actually a record of the political interests and power struggles that have shaped Canadian history and, therefore, your sense of who you are. Those who know how to read the census, and who understand something of its purpose and structure, can hear in the numbers the conflict of generations. Listen carefully enough and you may even hear an echo of your own struggles.

Jean Talon completed New France's first census of the population and its characteristics in 1666. The count: 3215—that is, 3215 French settlers. Talon did not count the much larger Aboriginal population, did not even try to estimate their number and socioeconomic characteristics. Of course, it would have been technically impossible for him to do so and prohibitively expensive even if it had been technically feasible. The Aboriginal population was, after all, nomadic, in part, and widely scattered in remote and often barely accessible regions. But the important point is that Talon wanted to count the colonists, not the Aboriginals. The first census was not a neutral count of all residents of New France but a means of providing information that could be used to help take control of the territory from the Aboriginals and establish a stable and prosperous French colony. Talon needed the numbers to rationalize the taxation of the French colonists, further their economic development, organize new colonization efforts, and, by implication, interfere with (and even destroy) the livelihoods and lives of the Aboriginal population. The fact that the Aboriginals weren't counted only added to the sense that they didn't count. In this way, the first census added to the mythology that New France was virgin territory, just waiting for European colonists to exploit its riches. Could there be a more political purpose?

For nearly two centuries following Talon's census, the authorities alone decided what was worth counting. The situation changed after the 1837 Rebellions. The people now wanted an elected government, and they wanted every citizen—or at least every male, non-Aboriginal citizen who owned property—to have equal say in whom their elected representatives would be. This change required not a repetition of the sporadic, regional censuses conducted to date, but a regular, nationwide census that would accurately count the population in specific geographic areas so that each member of the new Parliament would represent approximately the same number of citizens. The British North America Act, which established Canada in 1867, thus stipulated that a census would be conducted on a fixed date in the spring every 10 years (since 1956, every five years) and would count people in specific geographic areas. Again, the motive was political.

Recent censuses continue the tradition. Consider the ethnicity question. Ethnic and racial identities change over time, so census questions on race and ethnicity must change too. The 1931 census did not ask respondents to identify their ethnicity (the term was not yet commonly used) but rather their race. This way of classifying Canadians reflected racist theories of the time, which held that English, French, Chinese, Hungarians, and so on, were *biologically* different from one another. After the Nazi era, however, most people abandoned this unscientific and politically dangerous way of thinking about group differences. Instead, the census asked people to identify their *ancestry*. "To which ethnic or cultural group(s) did this person's ancestors belong?" asked the 1991 census.

The word "group(s)" is itself significant. Until 1981, the census obliged Canadians to specify a *single* ethnic or cultural origin. However, this neat pigeonholing proved unrealistic as more and more Canadians intermarried, underwent religious conversion, and became increasingly distant from their immigrant ancestors. What is the ancestry of a child born to a French Canadian who marries an English Canadian—French or English? What is the ancestry of a child born to a Dutch Protestant Canadian who marries a Polish-Jewish Canadian and then converts to Judaism—Dutch or Jewish? The answer is, of course, up to the respondent, but it was only in 1981 that he or she was allowed to say "both." Thus, from 1981 on, the census has allowed us not just to distinguish ethnic groups but to divide members of each group into "single response" and "multiple response" members. This distinction more accurately reflects the ethnic and cultural blending that is taking place in this country.

People who identified strongly with their ethnic group liked the ethnic question. After all, once Canada's multicultural policy was adopted in the early 1970s, federal money became available to support ethnic cultures. The overall amount of funding available depended largely on the significance of ethnicity in Canadian society as determined by the census. The amount of funding available to any one group depended on its size—again, as determined by the census. However, the ethnic question exaggerated size and therefore significance. It did this by not allowing respondents to claim they were "Canadian" by ancestry. The census forced Canadians to choose among various European, Asian, African, and other ancestries, even if they happened to be ninth-generation Canadians. Thus, the census exaggerated the multicultural nature of Canadian society and inflated the number of ethnic Canadians, a fact that pleased strong ethnic identifiers who wanted to promote their ethnic culture using federal funds.

Proof that the ethnic question exaggerated the multicultural nature of Canadian society came in 1996. Figure 1 shows the 1996 census question on ethnicity. "Canadian" is mentioned as a possible response for the first time. In fact, at midnight between May 13 and 14, 1996, Canada lost millions of citizens who had formerly specified European, Asian, African, and other ancestries, as "Canadian" became the most frequently chosen ethnic origin in the country. The census was finally accounting for the fact that millions of Canadians no longer thought of themselves as having a relevant ancestry that derived from foreign shores.

A relatively new census question about "visible minority" groups also reflects a new social reality with political overtones. Since the 1960s, Canada has welcomed many new immigrants from Asia, the Caribbean, and other non-traditional sources. Most of these new immigrants are not white. Hence the inclusion of a new question about visible minority status. Among other things, the data from this question allow the government to promote employment equity and prevent discrimination in hiring practices.

A last word on the politics of the ethnic question: The 2006 census incompletely enumerated 22 Indian reserves and settlements. The populations of these communities are not included in the census counts. Members of these reserves and settlements refused to participate in the census as an act of political protest. They simply do not recognize the authority of the federal government.

Figure 1
The Ethnicity Question on the 1996 Census

■ Source: Statistics Canada,
1996 Census of Population
Questionnaires: Long
Questionnaire. Question 17. Pg. 8.
Found at: http://www12.statcan.ca/
english/census01/info/96-2b-en.pdf.

To which ethnic or cultural group(s) did
this person's **ancestors** belong?

For example, French, English, German, Scottish,
Canadian, Italian, Irish, Chinese, Cree, Micmac,
Métis, Inuit (Eskimo), Ukrainian, Dutch, East Indian,
Polish, Portuguese, Jewish, Haitian, Jamaican,
Vietnamese, Lebanese, Chilean, Somali, etc.

Specify as many groups as applicable.

In the following pages, additional political aspects of the Canadian census will become evident. For example, you will learn that the average income of Canadian families (after taking inflation into account) has not changed much in decades. In Canada's universities, men and women tend to be concentrated in different fields that are associated with different income levels. The gap between the annual incomes of immigrants and non-immigrants is growing. These facts do not speak for themselves. Social scientific facts are always collected and interpreted with particular expectations and aims in mind. However, these facts are potentially incendiary bases for policy debate and action. What are your expectations and aims? Where do you fit into the politics of the 2006 census?

A Note on the Tables

The data in the following tables are mainly from the 2006 Census of Canada. Unless otherwise indicated, the data refer to citizens, landed immigrants, and non-permanent residents alive in Canada, as well as citizens and landed immigrants alive and temporarily residing outside Canada, on midnight between May 15 and 16, 2006. The census was administered on May 16, 2006.

A short questionnaire was distributed to 80 percent of Canadian households. A long questionnaire was distributed to the remaining 20 percent. Some of the tables below are based on 100 percent of respondents, others on the 20 percent sample.

The formatting of, and calculations in, the tables are mine.

Population Growth and Geographical Distribution

Table 1
Population by Province or Territory, 1996 and 2006

Province or Territory	Population, 1996	Percentage of Total, 1996	Population, 2006	Percentage of Total, 2006	Population Change, 1996–2006 (%)
Newfoundland and Labrador	551 795	1.9	505 469	1.6	−8.4
Prince Edward Island	134 555	0.5	135 851	0.4	1.0
Nova Scotia	909 280	3.2	913 462	2.9	0.5
New Brunswick	738 130	2.6	729 997	2.3	−1.1
Quebec	7 138 795	24.7	7 546 131	23.9	5.7
Ontario	10 753 575	37.3	12 160 282	38.5	13.1
Manitoba	1 113 900	3.9	1 148 401	3.6	3.1
Saskatchewan	990 240	3.4	968 157	3.1	−2.2
Alberta	2 696 825	9.3	3 290 350	10.4	22.0
British Columbia	3 724 500	12.9	4 113 487	13.0	10.4
Yukon	30 765	0.1	30 372	0.1	−1.3
Northwest Territories	64 400	0.2	41 464	0.1	*
Nunavut	*	*	29 474	0.1	*
Total	28 846 760	100.0	31 612 897	100.0	9.6

* Nunavut was officially separated from the Northwest Territories on April 1, 1999.

Source: Adapted from Statistics Canada, "Population and dwelling counts, for Canada, provinces and territories, 1991 and 1996 censuses - 100% data," Cat. No. 93-357-XPB. Found at: http://www.statcan.ca/english/census96/table1e.pdf; and Statistics Canada, "Population and dwelling counts, for Canada, provinces and territories, 2006 and 2001 censuses - 100% data." Found at: http://www12.statcan.ca/english/census06/data/popdwell/Table.cfm?T=101.

Canada's population was 31.6 million in 2006, having increased 9.6 percent since 2001 through "natural increase" (births) and immigration (Table 1). Among Canada's 13 provinces and territories, Alberta, Ontario, and British Columbia grew the most because they attracted the most immigrants and migrants from other parts of Canada. The populations of Newfoundland and Labrador, Saskatchewan, New Brunswick, and Yukon shrank, largely because economic opportunities in those jurisdictions were less attractive than economic opportunities elsewhere, thus encouraging people in their prime working years to migrate.

A census metropolitan area (CMA) is an area consisting of one or more neighbouring municipalities situated around a major urban core. A CMA must have a total population of at least 100 000, of which 50 000 or more live in the urban core. By this definition, there were 33 CMAs in Canada in 2006, the fastest growing of which were Barrie,

Calgary, Oshawa, Edmonton, Kelowna, Toronto, and Kitchener (Table 2). These seven CMAs are areas of rapid economic growth and attractiveness to internal migrants and new immigrants. For example, demand for oil spurred growth in Calgary and Edmonton; a high-technology boom (the BlackBerry and other innovations coming out of the University of Waterloo) made Kitchener a growth centre; and solid economic growth combined with large, established immigrant communities made Toronto and surrounding communities a magnet for new immigrants. Only two CMAs shrunk between 2001 and 2006: Saguenay and Saint John.

Table 2
Population by Census Metropolitan Area, 2006

CMA	Population, 2006	Population, 2001	Population Change (%)
1 Toronto (Ont.)	5 113 149	4 682 897	9.2
2 Montréal (Que.)	3 635 571	3 451 027	5.3
3 Vancouver (B.C.)	2 116 581	1 986 965	6.5
4 Ottawa–Gatineau (Ont./Que.)	1 130 761	1 067 800	5.9
5 Calgary (Alta.)	1 079 310	951 494	13.4
6 Edmonton (Alta.)	1 034 945	937 845	10.4
7 Quebec (Que.)	715 515	686 569	4.2
8 Winnipeg (Man.)	694 668	676 594	2.7
9 Hamilton (Ont.)	692 911	662 401	4.6
10 London (Ont.)	457 720	435 600	5.1
11 Kitchener (Ont.)	451 235	414 284	8.9
12 St. Catharines–Niagara (Ont.)	390 317	377 009	3.5
13 Halifax (N.S.)	372 858	359 183	3.8
14 Oshawa (Ont.)	330 594	296 298	11.6
15 Victoria (B.C.)	330 088	311 902	5.8
16 Windsor (Ont.)	323 342	307 877	5.0
17 Saskatoon (Sask.)	233 923	225 927	3.5
18 Regina (Sask.)	194 971	192 800	1.1
19 Sherbrooke (Que.)	186 952	175 950	6.3
20 St. John's (N.L.)	181 113	172 918	4.7
21 Barrie (Ont.)	177 061	148 480	19.2
22 Kelowna (B.C.)	162 276	147 739	9.8
23 Abbotsford (B.C.)	159 020	147 370	7.9
24 Greater Sudbury/Grand Sudbury (Ont.)	158 258	155 601	1.7
25 Kingston (Ont.)	152 358	146 838	3.8
26 Saguenay (Que.)	151 643	154 938	−2.1
27 Trois-Rivières (Que.)	141 529	137 507	2.9
28 Guelph (Ont.)	127 009	117 344	8.2
29 Moncton (N.B.)	126 424	118 678	6.5
30 Brantford (Ont.)	124 607	118 086	5.5
31 Thunder Bay (Ont.)	122 907	121 986	0.8
32 Saint John (N.B.)	122 389	122 678	−0.2
33 Peterborough (Ont.)	116 570	110 876	5.1

Age Distribution

Demographers invented the term *population pyramid* to describe age-sex distributions that were wide at the base and narrow at the top. Aging populations in economically developed countries started to change the shape of age-sex distributions—narrowing the base, widening the peak—and the baby boomers (born between 1946 and 1965) turned them into something resembling a spinning top (Figure 2). The baby boomers are now starting to retire, and as they do, they are putting increasing strain on the pension and health care systems, which are funded largely out of taxes paid by Canadians in their prime working years. Some social scientists have asked a good question: Will the spinning top get so top-heavy that it becomes unstable?

Figure 2
Population Pyramid, 2006

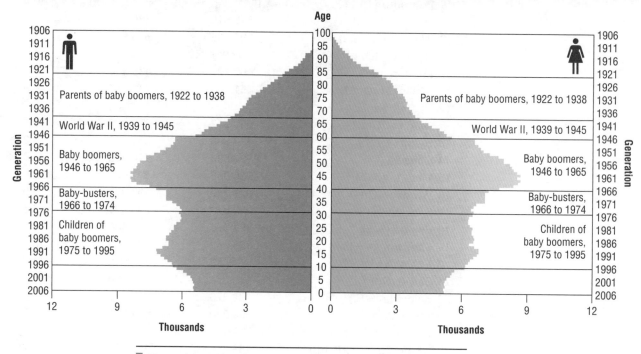

Source: Adapted from Statistics Canada 2006 Census. Found at: http://www12.statcan.ca/census-recensement/2006/rt-td/index-eng.cfm.

The graph of the mean (or average) age of Canadians from 1956 to 2006 is shaped like a hockey stick (Figure 3). The blade reflects the birth of the baby boomers. The handle reflects the post-1965 aging of the population because of Canadian women having fewer children (because of women's mass entry into the paid labour force and the widespread availability of contraception), improved nutrition, a 50 percent decline in the number of smokers, and various medical advances.

Figure 3
Mean Age of Canadians 1956–2006

■ Source: Adapted from Statistics Canada 2006 Census. Found at: http://www12.statcan.ca/census-recensement/2006/rt-td/index-eng.cfm.

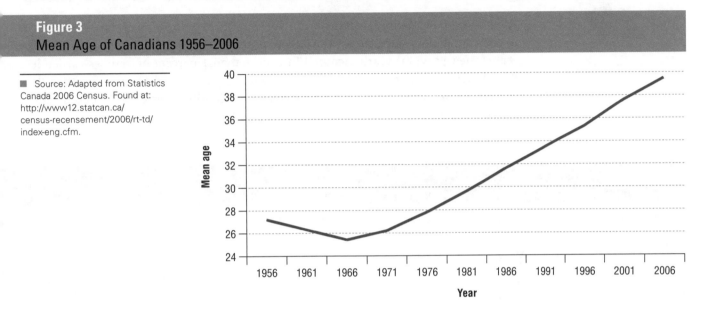

Income and Labour Force Activity

After taxes, mean family income in Canada was $67 649 in 2005, up just 11.1 percent in constant dollars since 1980. (The dollar amounts are for 2005 because people had to report their previous year's income.) Just more than 1 percent of families earned less than $5000 in that year (Figure 4); on average, they borrowed $1604 more than they earned. At the other extreme, nearly 9 percent of families earned $150 000 or more. The average income of these families was $187 422.

Figure 4
Mean Total Family After-Tax Income by Income Category, 2005

Notes: Category percentages do not add to 100 percent because of rounding. The numbers above the bars are the income category as a percentage of all families.

■ Source: Adapted from Statistics Canada 2006 Census. Found at: http://www12.statcan.ca/census-recensement/2006/rt-td/index-eng.cfm.

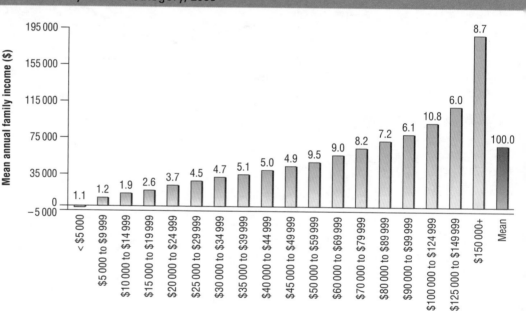

Women's labour force participation rate (the proportion of people 15 years and over working in the paid labour force) has been rising steadily since the beginning of the twentieth century and declining more or less steadily for men since World War II. Table 3 shows that the trend continued up to 2006, when 72.3 percent of men and 61.6 percent of women worked in the paid labour force. The long-term trend in the unemployment rate was upward from the 1940s to the 1990s and downward thereafter. Table 3 captures the trend over the past three decades, with the 2006 unemployment rate for men at 6.5 percent for men and 6.6 percent for women—figures not seen in Canada since the 1960s.

Table 3
Population 15 Years and Over by Labour Force Activity and Sex, 1986–2006

	1986		1996		2006	
	Male	**Female**	**Male**	**Female**	**Male**	**Female**
Unemployment rate (%)	9.6	11.2	10.2	10.0	6.5	6.6
Participation rate (%)	77.5	55.9	72.7	58.6	72.3	61.6

Source: Adapted from Statistics Canada 2006 Census. Found at: http://www12.statcan.ca/census-recensement/2006/rt-td/index-eng.cfm.

Women and men are distributed differently in the Canadian occupational structure, and, in many cases, the narrower the occupational category, the more marked the differences. Consider a broad occupational category, such as "sales and service occupations." Of the workers who fall into this category, 57.5 percent are women, while 42.5 percent are men: a difference of 15 percent (Table 4). One of the narrow occupational categories within sales and service occupations is "cashiers." Some 85.2 percent of cashiers are women, compared with just 14.8 percent of men: a difference of 70.4 percent.

For decades, women have been entering occupations that were traditionally heavily male-dominated, but Table 4 shows that progress has been less dramatic than many people believe. Men still dominate in blue-collar occupations and occupations that command relatively high pay and are associated with relatively high levels of authority and prestige, especially those requiring scientific and technical skills. Women still dominate in service occupations: teaching below the university level, nursing, social work, secretarial and clerical work, and so on.

Among Canadians who work full-time and year-round, income increased only modestly between 2000 and 2005. (The 2001 census asked about income in 2000, the 2006 census about income in 2005.) The improvement was somewhat better for women (3.9 percent) than for men (2.5 percent), but the gap between women's and men's income remained substantial (Table 5). In 2005, women earned just 77 percent of what men earned, reflecting the fact that women are concentrated in occupations that are valued less highly than the jobs in which men are concentrated.

Table 4

Labour Force 15 Years and Over by Occupation and Sex, 2006

Occupation	Male (%)	Female (%)
Management occupations	63.3	36.7
Senior management occupations	*76.2*	*23.8*
Business, finance, and administrative occupations	28.5	71.5
Secretaries	*2.1*	*97.9*
Clerical occupations	*28.4*	*71.6*
Natural and applied sciences and related occupations	78.1	21.9
Health occupations	19.9	80.1
Physicians, dentists, and veterinarians	*63.4*	*36.6*
Nurse supervisors and registered nurses	*6.3*	*93.7*
Occupations in social science, education, government service, and religion	31.9	68.1
Judges	*75.4*	*24.6*
Lawyers and Quebec notaries	*61.4*	*38.6*
Psychologists	*29.5*	*70.5*
Social workers	*18.4*	*81.6*
University professors	*61.1*	*38.9*
Secondary school teachers	*42.7*	*57.3*
Elementary school and kindergarten teachers	*16.4*	*83.6*
Occupations in art, culture, recreation, and sport	44.9	55.1
Sales and service occupations	42.5	57.5
Cashiers	*14.8*	*85.2*
Trades, transport, and equipment operators and related occupations	93.1	6.9
Occupations unique to primary industry	77.7	22.3
Occupations unique to processing, manufacturing, and utilities	66.7	33.3
Total labour force	52.6	47.4

Source: Adapted from Statistics Canada 2006 Census. Found at: http://www12.statcan.ca/census-recensement/2006/rt-td/index-eng.cfm.

Table 5

Median Annual Income in Constant (2005) Dollars for Full-Year, Full-Time Earners, by Sex, and Female–Male Earnings Ratio, 2000 and 2005

Male			Female			Female–Male Ratio		
2000	2005	Change	2000	2005	Change	2000	2005	Change
$45 654	$46 778	2.5%	$34 488	$35 830	3.9%	0.76	0.77	0.01

Source: Adapted from Statistics Canada 2006 Census. Found at: http://www12.statcan.ca/census-recensement/2006/rt-td/index-eng.cfm.

Unpaid domestic work was officially invisible until Statistics Canada started asking questions about it a few censuses ago. We now know precisely how domestically overworked women are. For Canadians who spend few hours per week on housework, child care, and senior care, the difference between women and men is small, but among those who spend many hours per week on these forms of domestic work, the difference is huge (Figure 5). Consider Canadians who spend 60 hours a week or more on child care. Three-quarters of them are women and one-quarter of them are men. For Canadians who spend 60 hours a week or more on care of older adults (seniors), the proportions are the same. Overall, female-male differences in hours of domestic work are biggest for senior care and smallest for child care.

Figure 5
Weekly Hours of Unpaid Work by Sex, for Population 15 Years and Over, 2006

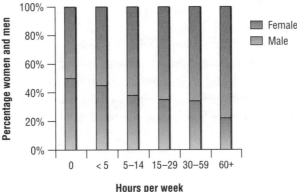

Source: Adapted from Statistics Canada 2006 Census. Found at: http://www12.statcan.ca/census-recensement/2006/rt-td/index-eng.cfm.

Ethnicity, Visible Minority Status, and Aboriginal Status

Census respondents can specify more than one ethnic membership. Accordingly, Table 6 lists the 35 most numerous ethnic groups in Canada by single and multiple responses. We may calculate a crude index of assimilation into Canadian society by dividing the single responses for each ethnic group by the number of multiple responses for that group. The index implies that as people assimilate, they are more likely to intermarry, undergo religious conversion, identify less strongly with their ancestors' country of origin, and therefore express multiple ethnic identities. The higher the index, the less assimilated the group. For all Canadians, the index of assimilation is 1.4, which means that Canadians are 40 percent more likely to express single than multiple ethnic origins. For Korean Canadians, the corresponding figure is 15.7, which means that Korean Canadians are 1570 percent more likely to say they are Korean than Korean and some other ethnicity. Chinese, East Indian, Vietnamese, and Filipino Canadians also score high on the index. This suggests that recency of immigration and non-European origin are associated with high scores on the index, that is, low levels of assimilation.

Statistics Canada classifies members of visible minority groups as people, other than Aboriginal Canadians, who define themselves as "non-Caucasian in race or non-white in colour." About a seventh of Canadians—more than 5 million people—are members of visible minority groups. The provinces with the largest visible minority populations (around a fifth to a quarter of the total population) are British Columbia and Ontario (Table 7). Alberta, Manitoba, and Quebec have substantial visible minority populations (around a tenth to a seventh of the total population). Other provinces and territories have small visible minority populations (around a hundredth to a twentieth of the total population).

South Asians, Chinese, Blacks, Filipinos, Latin Americans, and Southeast Asians are the largest visible minority groups in Canada, but they are unevenly distributed across the country (Table 8). Obvious examples are the relatively large number of Chinese and small number of black people in British Columbia, the relatively large number of black people in Nova Scotia, and the relatively large number of Filipinos in Manitoba.

Table 6
Thirty-Five Largest Ethnic Groups, 2006

Ethnicity	Total Responses	Single Responses	Multiple Responses	Single Responses as Proportion of Multiple Responses
Canadian	10 066 290	5 748 725	4 317 570	1.3
English	6 570 015	1 367 125	5 202 890	0.3
French	4 941 210	1 230 535	3 710 675	0.3
Scottish	4 719 850	568 515	4 151 340	0.1
Irish	4 354 155	491 030	3 863 125	0.1
German	3 179 425	670 640	2 508 785	0.3
Italian	1 445 335	741 045	704 285	1.1
Chinese	1 346 510	1 135 365	211 145	5.4
North American Indian	1 253 615	512 150	741 470	0.7
Ukrainian	1 209 085	300 590	908 495	0.3
Dutch (Netherlands)	1 035 965	303 400	732 560	0.4
Polish	984 565	269 375	715 190	0.4
East Indian	962 665	780 175	182 495	4.3
Russian	500 600	98 245	402 355	0.2
Welsh	440 965	27 115	413 855	0.1
Filipino	436 190	321 390	114 800	2.8
Norwegian	432 515	44 790	387 725	0.1
Portuguese	410 850	262 230	148 625	1.8
Métis	409 065	77 295	331 770	0.2
British Isles n.i.e.*	403 915	94 145	309 770	0.3
Swedish	334 765	28 445	306 325	0.1
Spanish	325 730	67 475	258 255	0.3
American	316 350	28 785	287 565	0.1
Hungarian (Magyar)	315 510	88 685	226 820	0.4
Jewish	315 120	134 045	181 070	0.7
Greek	242 685	145 250	97 435	1.5
Jamaican	231 110	134 320	96 785	1.4
Danish	200 035	33 770	166 265	0.2
Austrian	194 255	27 060	167 195	0.2
Romanian	192 170	79 650	112 515	0.7
Vietnamese	180 125	136 445	43 685	3.1
Belgian	168 910	33 670	135 240	0.2
Lebanese	165 150	103 855	61 295	1.7
Québécois	146 585	96 835	49 750	1.9
Korean	146 550	137 790	8 755	15.7
Total**	31 241 030	18 319 580	12 921 445	1.4

* n.i.e. = not included elsewhere
** Including ethnic groups not listed here
Note: In some cases, Total Responses do not equal Single Responses plus Multiple Responses because Statistics Canada reports figures rounded off to multiples of 5.

Source: Adapted from Statistics Canada 2006 Census. Found at: http://www12.statcan.ca/census-recensement/2006/rt-td/index-eng.cfm.

Table 7
Visible Minority Population by Province or Territory, 2006

	Total Population	Visible Minority Population	Visible Minority Population as % of Total
Newfoundland and Labrador	500 605	5 720	1.1
Prince Edward Island	134 205	1 830	1.4
Nova Scotia	903 090	37 680	4.2
New Brunswick	719 650	13 345	1.9
Quebec	7 435 905	654 355	8.8
Ontario	12 028 895	2 745 205	22.8
Manitoba	1 133 510	109 095	9.6
Saskatchewan	953 845	33 900	3.6
Alberta	3 256 355	454 200	13.9
British Columbia	4 074 385	1 008 855	24.8
Yukon	30 195	1 220	4.0
Northwest Territories	41 060	2 270	5.5
Nunavut	29 325	420	1.4
Total	31 241 030	5 068 090	16.2

Source: Adapted from Statistics Canada 2006 Census. Found at: http://www12.statcan.ca/census-recensement/2006/rt-td/index-eng.cfm.

Table 8
Visible Minority Groups as a Percentage of Provincial or Territorial Population, 2006

	South Asian*	Chinese	Black	Filipino	Latin American	Southeast Asian**
Newfoundland and Labrador	0.3	0.3	0.2	0.1	0.1	0.0
Prince Edward Island	0.1	0.2	0.5	0.0	0.2	0.0
Nova Scotia	0.4	0.5	2.1	0.1	0.1	0.1
New Brunswick	0.3	0.3	0.6	0.1	0.1	0.1
Quebec	1.0	1.1	2.5	0.3	1.2	0.7
Ontario	6.6	4.8	3.9	1.7	1.2	0.9
Manitoba	1.5	1.2	1.4	3.3	0.6	0.5
Saskatchewan	0.5	1.0	0.5	0.4	0.3	0.3
Alberta	3.2	3.7	1.4	1.6	0.8	0.9
British Columbia	6.4	10.0	0.7	2.2	0.7	1.0
Yukon	0.6	1.1	0.4	0.7	0.3	0.5
Northwest Territories	0.5	0.8	0.9	1.7	0.2	0.9
Nunavut	0.3	0.3	0.3	0.3	0.1	0.0
Canada	4.0	3.9	2.5	1.3	1.0	0.8
Total	1 262 865	1 216 570	783 795	410 695	304 245	239 935

* South Asian = East Indian, Pakistani, Sri Lankan, etc.
** Southeast Asian = Vietnamese, Cambodian, Malaysian, Laotian, etc.

Source: Adapted from Statistics Canada 2006 Census. Found at: http://www12.statcan.ca/census-recensement/2006/rt-td/index-eng.cfm.

Aboriginal Canadians constitute 3.8 percent of Canada's population, but in the three northern territories, they represent 25 percent (Yukon), 50 percent (Northwest Territories), and 85 percent (Nunavut) of the total (Figure 6). Among the provinces, Manitoba and Saskatchewan have the largest Aboriginal populations in relative terms— about a seventh of the total population. Roughly 1 in 20 people living in Alberta, British Columbia, and Newfoundland and Labrador is an Aboriginal Canadian, while in the other provinces, the figure is between 1 percent and 3 percent.

Figure 6
Aboriginal Population by Province and Territory, 2006

Note: The numbers above the bars are the Aboriginal populations as a percentage of the provincial or territorial populations

■ Source: Adapted from Statistics Canada 2006 Census. Found at: http://www12.statcan.ca/census-recensement/2006/rt-td/index-eng.cfm.

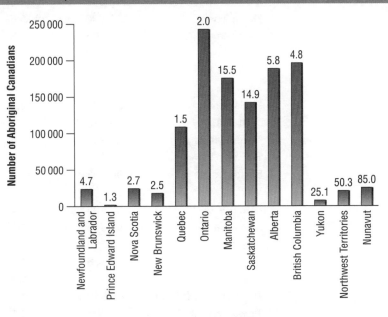

Immigrants accounted for 19.6 percent of Canada's population in 2006. In recent decades, that number has been increasing. At the same time, the source countries for Canada's immigrant population have changed dramatically (Table 9). The biggest shift has been from European to Asian sources. For example, although the biggest group of Canadian immigrants comes from the United Kingdom, they represented 15.1 percent of all immigrants before 1991 and just 2.3 percent of immigrants between 2001 and 2006. Meanwhile, Chinese represented just 3.9 percent of immigrants before 1991 but 14.0 percent between 2001 and 2006. Similarly, India and the Philippines have grown in importance as source countries, while Italy, Germany, Poland, and Portugal have declined.

Table 9
Immigrant Population by Country of Origin, Before 1991 and 2001–2006

Place of Birth	Immigrant Population	Immigrant Population (%)	Before 1991 (%)	2001–2006 (%)*
United Kingdom	579 620	9.4	15.1	2.3
China	466 940	7.5	3.9	14.0
India	443 690	7.2	4.6	11.6
Philippines	303 195	4.9	3.2	7.0
Italy	296 850	4.8	8.5	0.2
United States	250 535	4.0	5.0	3.5
Hong Kong	215 430	3.5	3.2	0.7
Germany	171 405	2.8	4.4	0.7
Poland	170 490	2.8	3.6	0.6
Vietnam	160 170	2.6	3.2	1.0
Portugal	150 390	2.4	4.0	0.3
Pakistan	133 280	2.2	0.6	5.2
Jamaica	123 420	2.0	2.5	0.8
Netherlands	111 990	1.8	3.0	0.3
Sri Lanka	105 670	1.7	0.7	2.0
South Korea	98 395	1.6	0.8	3.2
Iran	92 090	1.5	0.7	2.5
Guyana	87 195	1.4	1.7	0.7
Romania	82 645	1.3	0.7	2.5
France	79 550	1.3	1.3	1.5
Lebanon	75 275	1.2	1.2	1.0
Greece	73 125	1.2	2.0	0.1
Trinidad and Tobago	65 540	1.1	1.3	0.4
Taiwan	65 205	1.1	0.4	1.0
Russia	64 130	1.0	0.4	1.9
Haiti	63 350	1.0	1.0	1.0
Ukraine	59 460	1.0	0.7	1.4
Mexico	49 925	0.8	0.6	1.5
Hungary	45 940	0.7	1.1	0.2
El Salvador	42 780	0.7	0.7	0.3
Egypt	40 575	0.7	0.6	0.6
Croatia	39 250	0.6	0.8	0.1
Colombia	39 145	0.6	0.2	2.3
Morocco	39 055	0.6	0.4	1.3
South Africa	38 305	0.6	0.6	0.6
Other	1 262 940	20.4	17.3	25.7
Total	6 186 950	100.0	100.0	100.0

* Includes immigrants who landed in Canada before Census Day, May 16, 2006

Source: Adapted from Statistics Canada 2006 Census. Found at: http://www12.statcan.ca/census-recensement/2006/rt-td/index-eng.cfm.

Figure 7

Ratio of Recent Immigrant Earners' Median Annual Income to Canadian-Born
Earners' Median Annual Income, by University Education and Sex

■ Source: Adapted from Statistics
Canada 2006 Census. Found at:
http://www12.statcan.ca/
census-recensement/2006/rt-td/
index-eng.cfm.

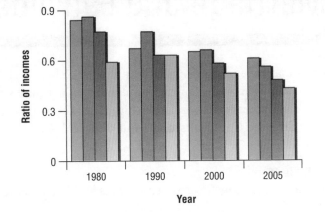

Men without university degree
Women without university degree
Men with university degree
Women with university degree

Comparing the median annual income of Canadian immigrants with the median annual income of people born in Canada over time reveals a troubling story. (The median separates the top from the bottom half of cases.) Each set of bars in Figure 7 is lower than the preceding set, indicating that the ratio of immigrants' to non-immigrants' income fell steadily between 1980 and 2005. In 1980, immigrants earned roughly 75 percent as much as non-immigrants earned. By 2005, they earned only about 55 percent as much.

Interestingly, the ratio of immigrant to non-immigrant income is higher for people without a university degree than for people with a university degree. In relative terms, highly educated immigrants are faring more poorly than less well-educated immigrants are. This finding suggests that Canada is doing a bad job of integrating well-educated immigrants into its economy. We must seek ways of improving the selection of university-educated immigrants and facilitating the upgrading of their skills and their accreditation once they arrive in Canada. Failure to do so could eventually produce a frustrated, marginalized, and radicalized immigrant community that resembles those in the United Kingdom and France rather than the well-integrated immigrant community to which Canadians have grown accustomed.

Marriage and Families

Legal marriage is less popular than it used to be, especially in Quebec. Common-law relationships are increasingly popular. About a fifth of single Canadians over the age of 14 are in a common-law relationship, as are about a sixth of separated Canadians, 3 out of 10 divorced Canadians, and 1 out of 20 widowed Canadians (Table 10).

Table 10
Marital Status by Common-Law Status for Population 15 and Over, 2006

Marital Status	Not in a Common-Law Relationship (%)	In a Common-Law Relationship (%)	Total (%)
Single	79.1	20.9	100.0
Married	100.0	0.0	100.0
Separated	83.2	16.8	100.0
Divorced	70.0	30.0	100.0
Widowed	95.4	4.6	100.0

Source: Adapted from Statistics Canada 2006 Census. Found at: http://www12.statcan.ca/census-recensement/2006/rt-td/index-eng.cfm.

On July 20, 2005, Canada became the fourth country in the world to legalize same-sex marriage. (The Netherlands, Belgium, and Spain preceded Canada, and South Africa and Norway are so far the only other countries to recognize same-sex marriage.) In the 10 months following the legalization of same-sex marriage in Canada, 7460 Canadians married people of the same sex, about half of them in Ontario and about a sixth in each of Quebec and British Columbia. In May 2006, nearly 38 000 Canadians were in same-sex, common-law relationships, with about a third of the total in each of Ontario and Quebec and a seventh in British Columbia. Altogether, the 45 350 Canadians in same-sex unions in 2006 represented 0.32 percent of non-single Canadians over the age of 14 who were married and in common-law unions (Table 11).

Table 11
Same-Sex Couples by Type of Union, Sex, and Province or Territory, 2006

	Same-Sex Couples			Same-Sex Married Couples			Same-Sex Common-Law Couples		
	Total	Male	Female	Total	Male	Female	Total	Male	Female
Newfoundland and Labrador	305	140	170	55	35	15	255	100	155
Prince Edward Island	140	45	100	20	10	15	125	40	85
Nova Scotia	1 255	590	665	140	70	70	1 115	520	595
New Brunswick	770	345	425	125	70	50	645	270	370
Quebec	13 685	7 920	5 765	1 255	690	570	12 425	7 230	5 195
Ontario	17 510	9 720	7 795	3 765	2 025	1 740	13 745	7 695	6 050
Manitoba	935	430	505	100	45	55	835	385	450
Saskatchewan	565	255	305	100	60	40	465	195	270
Alberta	3 055	1 535	1 520	510	270	240	2 545	1 265	1 275
British Columbia	7 035	3 745	3 295	1 370	735	635	5 665	3 010	2 660
Yukon	25	0	20	0	0	0	20	10	15
Northwest Territories	40	0	35	15	10	15	25	0	25
Nunavut	15	10	0	0	0	10	10	10	10
Canada	45 350	24 740	20 610	7 460	4 010	3 455	37 885	20 730	17 155

Source: Adapted from Statistics Canada 2006 Census. Found at: http://www12.statcan.ca/census-recensement/2006/rt-td/index-eng.cfm.

In 2006, more than two-thirds of Canadian families included a married couple, about a sixth included a common-law couple, and about a sixth were lone-parent families —more than 80 percent of which were headed by a woman (Figure 8). By definition, all lone-parent families had at least one child living at home, but among married-couple families, 56 percent had children living at home while among common-law couples just 45 percent had children living at home.

Figure 8
Family Structure, 2006

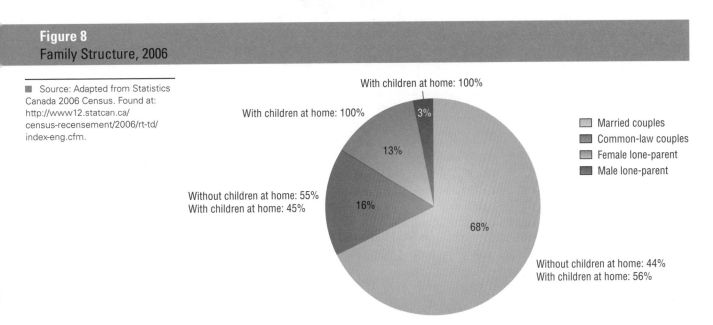

■ Source: Adapted from Statistics Canada 2006 Census. Found at: http://www12.statcan.ca/census-recensement/2006/rt-td/index-eng.cfm.

With children at home: 100%

With children at home: 100%

Without children at home: 55%
With children at home: 45%

3%

13%

16%

68%

☐ Married couples
☐ Common-law couples
☐ Female lone-parent
☐ Male lone-parent

Without children at home: 44%
With children at home: 56%

Education

The prime working-age population consists of people between the ages of 25 and 64. In 2006, almost a quarter of these people had a bachelor's degree or higher, while a quarter had a college or CEGEP degree or a university degree below the bachelor's level (Figure 9). One out of eight had earned an apprenticeship or trades certificate or diploma, while four out of ten had a high school or lower education.

Figure 9
Highest Level of Educational Attainment for Population Aged 25 to 64, 2006

Note: CEGEP stands for Collège d'enseignement général et professionnel. In Quebec, students attend CEGEPs before entering university or pursuing a trade.

■ Source: Adapted from Statistics Canada 2006 Census. Found at: http://www12.statcan.ca/census-recensement/2006/rt-td/index-eng.cfm

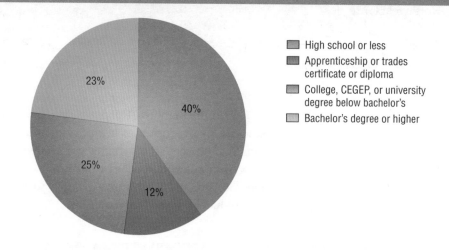

■ High school or less
■ Apprenticeship or trades certificate or diploma
■ College, CEGEP, or university degree below bachelor's
□ Bachelor's degree or higher

Although more women than men are now registered as students in Canadian universities, fewer women than men earn postgraduate degrees, and women tend to study in fields that lead them to jobs with lower pay and less power and prestige (Table 12). Thus, the ratio of men to women increases as we move from those who completed a bachelor's degree to those who completed a Ph.D. Moreover, the ratio of men to women is lowest in education, the visual and performing arts and communications technologies, and the humanities. It is highest in architecture; engineering and related technologies; personal, protective, and transportation services; and mathematics, computer, and information sciences. Clearly, the traditional division of labour is alive and well and living in Canada's institutions of higher learning.

Table 12
Ratio of Men to Women by Major Field of Study and Highest Degree Attained, for Population 15 and Over, 2006

Field of Study	Bachelor's	Master's	Ph.D.
Education	0.34	0.67	0.95
Visual and performing arts and communications technologies	0.56	0.70	1.11
Humanities	0.58	0.98	1.73
Social and behavioural sciences and law	0.74	0.82	1.43
Business, management, and public administration	1.04	1.53	1.97
Physical and life sciences and technologies	1.04	1.19	2.85
Mathematics, computer, and information sciences	2.13	1.22	4.16
Architecture, engineering, and related technologies	4.90	3.99	7.47
Agriculture, natural resources, and conservation	1.67	1.46	3.33
Health, parks, recreation, and fitness	0.28	0.43	1.66
Personal, protective, and transportation services	2.96	3.81	7.33
Other fields of study	0.44	0.85	0.55

Source: Adapted from Statistics Canada 2006 Census. Found at: http://www12.statcan.ca/census-recensement/2006/rt-td/index-eng.cfm.